UNHEARD

REAL OR STORY

ABHISHEK RAWAT

Made with ♥ on the Notion Press Platform
www.notionpress.com

Contents

Acknowledgements

I would like to thank the almighty for his blessings and giving me the power and zeal for the completion of this book. I would also like to thank my parents for having trust and encouraging me in my every step of life, without which I would have not been able to complete this book.

About The Author

Born and brought up in Prayagraj, Abhishek Rawat is a co-author of more than 10 anthologies and has worked with more than 3 publishing houses. A tax advisor by profession and a writer at heart, he believes that feelings are best expressed with words. Unheard- Real or Story, is his first solo book as an author. With this book, he has taken a step towards keeping one more foot inside the writing community world and sharing his imagination and feelings with the readers.

About Editor

DR. SUNIL PATIL

- नाम:- डॉ. सुनील पाटिल
- जन्म:- नीमच (मध्यप्रदेश)
- मात्रभाषा: - मराठी
- शिक्षा:- एम. ए. (हिंदी), एम.फिल. (हिंदी), बी.ए. (हिंदी), पीएच.डी. (हिंदी)
- तकनीकी शिक्षा: अनुवाद एवं पत्रकारिता में स्नातकोत्तर डिप्लोमा
- संप्रति: हिंदी प्रवक्ता, द्वारकादास गोवर्धनदास वैष्णव कॉलेज

(साय) , चेन्नई -600106.

- भाषाओं का ज्ञान:- हिंदी, हिंदी,तमिल,अंग्रेजी
- सम्मान:

• वर्ष 2016 लायंस क्लब इंटरनेशनल परेमिंड द्वारा बेस्ट टीचर अवार्ड प्राप्त।

- विलक्षाणा एक सार्थक पहल समिति अजायब (हरियाणा) द्वारा विलक्षणा शोध रतन सम्मान -2021
- विलक्षाणा एक सार्थक पहल समिति अजायब (हरियाणा) द्वारा आचार्य चाणक्य सम्मान-2021

● बोहल शोध मज्जूषा द्वारा इन्टरनेशनल टीचर्स प्राइड अवार्ड 2021

• एम.ए. (हिंदी) स्वर्ण पदक प्राप्त (उब शिक्षा और शोध संस्थान, दक्षिण भारत हिन्दी प्रचार सभा की चारों शाखाओं में प्रथम)
• राष्ट्रीय एवं अन्तर्राष्ट्रीय पत्र-पत्रिकाओं में शोधलेख प्रकाशित

ई-मेल : sunilpatil7969@gmail.com

Thought

ALWAYS REMEMBER
WHEN A MOTHER SAYS TO HER CHILD- "I LOVE YOU. YOU CAN NEVER DO ANY WRONG", SHE TRUSTS YOU AND BELIEVES IN YOU.

From The Author

"Yaar, kucch bhi kaho, maa is undoubtedly our best friend. Saara pyar ek taraf aur maa ki mamta ek taraf. Bilkul selfless, bina kisi expectation k wo din raat apne baccho k hi bare me, unke acche k liye hi sochti hai."

"Haan yaar sahi kaha tumne, but aaj tu itna emotional kyun ho raha hai? Baat kya hai?"

"Yaar kal Mother's Day hai aur life me pehli baar maa se itna dur hu isiliye thoda emotional ho gaya"

"Koi baat nahi, kal to jar raha hai na ghar, saari kasar nikal lena sabse dur rehne ki"

A usual day at London University with not such a usual day for Art faculty final year students as it is their last day in the university and all have gathered for their final submission of their yearly project report of the subject. It was quite noisy from the usual days as everyone was busy collecting one last time the memories they will be taking from here when they move on to their next phase of life. Sanjay and Vikram, were one of the students among those, chatting along about the memories they had with their family and excited to meet them after such a long time.

"Good morning everyone." Mr. Elfinston, H.O.D. of the Arts Department enters the room. "I hope you have your projects ready to be submitted so that you can get good grades in your final assessment".

"Yes Sir", out came a loud noise from everyone in assurance.

"Good, and by the way I wish you all a happy and a successful life ahead. May you all achieve success in your lives and make the institute proud."

"Thank You Sir".

"And one more thing. Wishing everyone's mother a very happy mother's day."

"So, since today is the last day of you all in this institute, I don't want to bore you all with my lecture but instead would like to tell you a story, a story of a mother. And by the end of it, it will be you as listeners to decide the fate of the story as I won't be raising questions neither questioning about the characters, but it is up to you all to decide according to your sensibility, what should be the end."

Everyone was excited to hear the story. Maybe more because they will not be listening to a boring bookish lecture for about an hour or more on the last day.

"So, the story is of Derbyshire village, a place far from city with some thousand people as residents, a story some 20 years back.......

CHAPTER ONE

THE ARRIVAL

"Daddy watch it". Suddenly the car came to a screeching halt.

"Sorry, I didn't saw it coming. Are you alright?"

"I'm fine dad, its just that I don't my drawing to look ugly because of your rash driving with my coloring pens scratching here and there in my drawing"

"What happened, Did I missed something?" – David from backseat of the car said.

" No, but you would have missed, if dad wouldn't have applied brakes."

"Ha..Ha..Ha.. not so funny Clark, I said I didn't saw it coming and by the way how come a cat come on the road?".

"Dad, we are in the village not city, so you need to be more careful with the animals rather than traffic".

"Seems like you've become matured".

"Any doubt?"

Clark and David, 11 years old, the twin brothers of Casey(their mother) and Roger have always cherished the love of their parents though they are not together anymore, but it never felt for the two kids that that one's love was less than the other for the two. After the divorce or rather we could say the separation, Casey decided to live in

Derbyshire village, a dream home both Casey and Roger made when they were together, when love flourished and grew to its full, while Roger decided to move to the city. Both agreed to the thing that it will not affect any of the children and that both will get love of both the parents. Coming to Derbyshire, to live with their mother during summer holidays was one.

"So here we arrive."

The car stopped at the front gate of the wooden house with some wooden furniture at the front area, just in front of the door. The house looked a bit old but was well maintained, as could be said looking from outside. David opened the gate of the car and ran straight inside the house. "Why is it always me who has to carry bags. Isn't it his responsibility also?" Clark somewhat furious at the behavior of David, leaving behind all the bags and baggage for Clark to carry inside.

"Take out your bags from the back carefully and make sure you don't disturb your mom. She has told during the call that she had a face surgery, I told her to cancel the coming of yours here but she insisted that she is fine and wanted to meet you"

"Aren't you coming inside? Mom will be happy to see you"

"I'm fine from here, your mom might not be happy seeing me in"

And so it was Clark left alone outside to carry those heavy bags inside with his father leaving him outside the front gate.

"Mom, we have arrived. Mom....where are you?"

"Did you find mom?"

"No, I searched in the hall, in the kitchen but she wasn't there"

"Let's go to her room"

And the two went for the room. Clark was about to unlock the knob of the door of the room when Casey came from inside.

"Oh, sorry. I didn't heard the sound of the car. I was busy wrapping a gift for you" and she put forward a gift wrapped in golden cover.

"What's inside?"

"Open it, but first lets go to your room".

"Wow! An airplane! I always wanted that. Thanks mom"

"Your father told me that you wanted it. But since he was too busy in his work, I thought I should bring it for you. Now since you are going to spend your holidays here I should tell you few house rules which you must obey during your stay"

"What? House rules"- both David and Clark said together.

"Yes, just normal ones, like you are not going to enter in my room without my permission, no locking of doors, no going to the barn at the back and please keep the curtains on during the day, as the doctor has told me to keep off from sunlight till my face gets healed".

"What actually happened to your face mom? And why this mask"

"nothing... it's just a small surgery for the scars. Don't worry, the mask is to protect my face and as soon as it gets healed, I'll take it off"

"Mom, I've made something for you" delivering the drawing Clark made for Casey.

"Oh, thank you dear. It's really lovely. I'll keep it in my room".

"Now, get some sleep while I go out and bring some veggies for the dinner tonight, you must be hungry and tired by the journey"

"Aren't you forgetting something mom?"

"What?"

"You used to sing a special song to make us sleep. Don't you remember?"

"Clark you are 11 now and not a 5 or 6 year kid. Try to sleep. You'll feel good". And Casey comes out of the kid's room.

"How can mom forget the song?"- David said in an interrogative tone.

"She hasn't forgotten. Didn't you hear what she said? We are not small kids. Maybe she wants us to be independent."- Clark explained.

"Or maybe she doesn't loves us anymore. How long have we not met her, 2 year or more?"

"Shut up. And try to sleep".

Casey went to her room, poured some red wine in the glass and sat on a rocking chair enjoying the drink.

From the room next door, she could hear the song though not clearly, but the song she knew by heart

Lullaby and good night

You are your mother's delight,

Shining angels beside.....

CHAPTER TWO

A NEW DAY

"No wonder why mom chose to live here. It so lively here with no honking and noisy neighbors and such large field to play"

Both Clark and David were happy enjoying playing outside on a nice and warm sunny day which they rarely get in their city life. It was like a heaven for them and returning after more than a year long gap and playing like they used to, running around, when they were kids, was almost a treat for them.

"come and catch me if you can"

"you know you can't run faster than me....I'll catch you in minutes"

David ran after Clark, a run and chase game which everyone enjoys.

"Clark stop. Don't go inside the barn. Mom has told not to go inside. She'll get angry if she gets to know it"

"but why will she stop us from getting in there. Don't you want to find out"

"Maybe she hasn't cleaned it in a while and she doesn't want us to get dirty and increase her work load. What else could be the reason? haa...?"

"Or may be something else. Who knows. Lets find out. And who will tell her about it?"

And Clark went looking for something with which he could break the shackles of the door of the barn which were so weak already that it could have been broken had Clark would have used his powers if not all. David was standing at the front of the barn waiting for Clark.

"Gotch ya"- finding a hammer in the woods, which might have been left by Casey long ago and forgotten, Clark returned to open the gate.

"Now this should help"

"What the hell are you doing here? Didn't I told you that you are not supposed to be anywhere near the barn?"

Surprised by the sudden appearance of Casey while they were busy of finding out something precious, the hammer just slept from the hand of Clark.

"M..M..Mom nothing..w..w..we..we were just playing here"

"Your stammering itself tells what you were up to" and with a fit of rage she grabbed Clark's hand and twisted it a bit.

"I told you that till the time you are here, you need to follow certain rules. Didn't I??"

"Mom, please leave. It's hurting"

"You need to understand first that you are not a small boy anymore and that you need to take things and whatever I say, seriously"

Leaving his hand from her grip and kind of pushing him on the ground Casey made her way back to home while Clark got hurt during the process.

"Are you hurt?"- enquired David.

"Yeah,a bit. But why is mom behaving like this. It was just a barn."

"I told you, she doesn't love us anymore. Yesterday she forgot that she used to sing for us. Today she did this. Mom could never do this to us".

"What do you want to say?"

"Can't you see by yourself that she is behaving like a stranger to us. She never came to meet us in these 2-3 years..."

"She gave us present when we came"

"Even a stranger when meets for first time gives it"

"What exactly do you want to say?"

"I want to say that maybe she is not the same mom she used to be with us before or...."

"Or...what??"

"Or....maybe.....she is not our mom. Look how she behaves with us. Plus from the time we have come here, we have seen her in that stupid mask only."

"I think you are over reacting David. She told us that she had a surgery and doctor has advised her to keep it on."

"Well....you wish..."

"Ya"

"Let's go inside and get you some antiseptic cream or something and clean your wound. And remember, no matter what I'm always by your side. After all we are twins."

"Now that's my biggest problem"- and Clark ran inside laughing with David chasing after him.

CHAPTER THREE

THE BOGGLE

If a father gets angry, it is considered normal by the society, as he has many responsibilities, from managing work to managing home and various other things. It is thought that because of so much burden or responsibilities on his shoulders, he could sometimes be irritated or rather he attains a position where you cannot act funny or give a chance to someone else to be open with you, and it is sometimes, to a certain extent, considered normal. But it is not the case with the mother.

A mother, on the other hand, if gets angry, is expected to either give an explanation for her behavior or should be back to normal, pouring down her love on her children. Having an equal responsibility of managing work outside and at home, growing up children and other burdens, it is expected from her to have a smiling face all the time. And by chance if she happens to be in a bad mood for more than a day, she might become a villain for the whole house.

Ever since David and Clark arrived, Casey's behavior towards them was not what they remember, they have ever seen before. Making rules, ignoring talks and being harsh on her children, all these were enough for Casey to put under the scrutiny. The seed to suspect her has been put in the mind of Clark.

“You know what” Clark said to David while having toast and juice at the breakfast on the dinner table, “I gave a thought to what you said yesterday and decided that I must give a try.”

“Try....to what?”

“To, what you said yesterday”.

“So what are you going to do about it?”

“The only way to find out the answer is to go inside mom’s room”.

“Are you serious? Have you forgot what she did yesterday when we tried to open the barn. She’ll be even more furious if she finds out that we have entered her room without her permission”

“I know it’s risky but who’s going to tell, you?”

“Good morning Clark, what’s going on?”- Casey enters the dining area.

“Nothing mom, just having my breakfast”- Clark said making a poker face as if no talk was going on.

“Look, I’m really sorry dear for what I did yesterday. I know I shouldn’t be harsh to you but you need to understand that whatever I say to you or do, is for your betterment”.

“I understand mom, and I promise I will not do it again”

“Good now have your breakfast while I am going to the market for some groceries. Will bring some cup cakes and chocolates for you. Do you need anything else?”

“No mom”

“Bye honey, take care and remember, no mischief while I’m out”

“Don’t worry mom”

Casey gets the car keys and goes out.

“So what is your plan?”- David enquired.

"Nothing. We're just going inside the room and try to find out any evidence to prove what you said. If we find nothing, then she is our mother."

"what if we find something to prove that she is not?"

"We'll see"- and Clark walked towards the room as he had no answer to David's question at the moment.

They walked stifled as if they were robbers.

"You go and find something in that corner while I look here"

Sometimes between the fight of heart and mind, you always want the heart to win. Clark, though at first wanted to figure out whether what David said was true or not, but he wanted (or rather his heart wanted) to prove David's speculation to be wrong.

"Look what I found"- David from one corner of the room pointing at the dustbin.

Clark moved towards the dustbin with heavy legs and an unusual type of fear, which happens when someone doesn't want to face the reality.

Lying in the dustbin was the drawing which Clark had made and gifted Casey, torn from in between. Just like the torn pieces, it looked like the view made Clark's heart been torn apart. No more evidence required, no explanation needed. David was right. Cark quickly took those pieces from the dustbin and was about to leave when Casey entered the room.

"I told you not to enter my room without my permission, do I need to remind you every hour? Just a few minutes back, you felt sorry for your action and now you're repeating the same mistake again?" This time Casey couldn't control her anger and slapped him with a power enough to make Clark cry.

"You cannot command us to do things, you're not our mom" and Clark went to his room while Casey followed him.

"What?....What do you mean by that?"

"You're not our mom, you're an imposter. Our mom would never treat us the way you treat us"

"What wrong did I did to you? Beat you for not listening to what I said?"

"No, this"- and Clark showed the torn drawing.

"Listen....dear....I can explain it to you" Casey's anger suddenly disappeared realizing the situation.

"Just go away, I don't want to listen to anything"

Helpless, she walked out of the room.

Clark leaned on David's shoulder and cried while David consoled him. At this point of time, Clark thought that everyone else except David was against him. This was certainly going to be a long day for both the kids.

CHAPTER FOUR

THE ESCAPE

"Now what are we going to do?"

"We need to tell this to dad and ask for help from someone here, maybe the neighbors here in finding our mom".

"But the telephone is in mom's room and after what has happened, I don't think that she will let us enter the room, let alone make the call".

"We need to do it anyhow, if she doesn't let us enter the room, we'll go out to our neighbors and will call dad from there"

The plan was built and the only thing was to wait for the night, so that Casey does not gets to know what they were doing. They had to wait for her to go to her room. It was raining heavily that night and the electricity supply was disconnected. But they were determined to do what they had decided.

The village was not densely populated. The neighbors were friendly but not much interacted with other. Casey's house was at the end of the lane and the nearest neighbor lived some 100 meters away. Though not much of distance, but on that day, it was about 100 miles for Clark.

"Hello, is someone there? I'm Clark, your neighbor's son. Is someone there?" No response came from inside. The neighbors were out that was a bad news for Clark and David.

"Now what?"

"We should wait, who knows they might be somewhere around and might come back after sometime, it's raining anyways, they might be stuck somewhere".

Both took the shelter in the shade covering the front portion or the sitting area in front of the house.

"There you are. What are you doing here? Why you came out of the house when it was raining so much?"

A flash light of torch on the face disturbed the sleep of Clark. Waiting for the neighbors to come back, he slept inside the waiting area, outside the house.

"Answer me Clark. You know, it's because of you I had to come out in this heavy rain and because of that I had to remove the mask 4 days before the time doctor prescribed me to keep it on"

It was then Clark realized that her mother was without the mask, the root cause of their suspicion. It was their mom, yes it was their mom, Casey. But why was she behaving like that with them all these days, was still the question in his mind.

"Nothing, I just wanted to go out for a walk."

"In rain?"

"It wasn't raining when we went out. Suddenly it started raining and we took shelter here and were waiting for it to stop"

"Anyways, let's get back to home. You are completely drenched and will catch cold if you don't take them off and warm yourself"

Clark looked a bit hesitant to go with her, and so did David.

"Ok look I'm not going to beat or scold you for what you did today, but you need to hurry up and get home before you catch cold okay!"

They had no choice but to go with her. Unwillingly, they started to follow her back to the house.

Clark was in two minds. On hand, it was David's words and to some extent was right. The behavior of Casey, from the moment they had arrived, has been suspicious and unusual like they have never seen. All the restrictions, her rude behavior were all to put her in the custody of both the children's motherly grading system.

But at the same time it is her only, who is caring enough to come out, irrespective of her condition, to look out for her kids, forgetting their mischief and helping them with warmth, which only a mother could do.

Clark was in dilemma, whether to take any step regarding her previous actions or to forget everything.

(2)

"So, now do you believe her?"- David enquired.

"You too saw with your own eyes. She had her mask off, she is our mom. Is there anything to doubt?"

"it's not a rocket science now. All you need is to have a plastic surgery of your face and you can get anyone's face. I've seen movies. Plus did she gave any reason as to why she threw your drawing in the dustbin and why she has been behaving strange, she even doesn't knows the song she used to sing for us. Do you have any answer to this?"

"But why will she take place of our mom? What will she get by doing this?"

"Only she can tell. We need to find out. We don't even know in what situation our mom is, what she has done to her."

"But who is going to believe us? We are just 11 and people will think us as fools when they see her standing in front of us and we telling them that our mother has gone missing. We don't even have proof that whatever we are saying is true".

"Whatever it is, I am not going to stay here with her. Who knows she might kill us just to keep her secret."

"We can do one thing. She will not let us find mom if she is around. We need to find when she is not around."

"We have already tried that."

"This time it will be different."

CHAPTER FIVE

FACE OFF

The rain had stopped, it was already 7 in the morning and the sun was shining brightly. Casey was soon awaken with the curtains being rolled out of the window and Clark standing in front of her bed. She smiled looking at him and tried to get up but found it difficult. She found her hands and legs being duck taped with the corners of the bed.

"Clark, what's this? Is this some kind of a joke because I definitely don't like it."

"This is not a joke. We have done this so that this time you don't interrupt".

"Interrupt? In what?"

"In finding our mom"

"I am your mom"

"No, you're not. And stop acting like you are. You are an imposter who has kidnapped her and has taken her place".

"Who told you that? David?"

"Yes, I mean No. You are not our mom. You act strange, if you were our mom you wouldn't have treated us that way".

"I am your mom. How should I convince you?"

"The only way is tell us where you have kept our mom and we'll free you"

"How can I tell that when I am your mom and I'm right here in front of you. Please Clark let me loose, it's hurting"

"Nope. I'm not going to let you lose unless you tell us the truth".

"I am your mom and this is the only truth dear. Why will I kidnap myself?"

"Then tell us the truth"

"I am your mom. How should I make you believe?"

"Don't believe her Clark, let's go. We need to go to dad. Let him find the truth himself. Till then let her be like that. At least this should be her punishment for doing that". David was getting impatient and walked out.

"We are going to tell dad personally. Till then decide something good to tell dad why you did all this and where you have kept our mom."

Clark was about to leave the room when he heard something unexpected at that time.

"Lullaby, and good night,
You are your mother's delight,
Shining angels beside
My darling abide"- it was Casey singing lullaby she used to sing for her kids when they were small.

"Mom!"- Clark a bit stunned and shocked or whether realizing his mistake(only he can tell), ran towards her. He took a scissor from the drawer and cut the tape.

"I'm sorry mom, I'm really sorry. I didn't realized it was you. How could I do that to you. I'm really sorry mom" Clark sobbing while cutting the tapes.

"Shhshhh...listen listen. Clark, look at me. Its ok dear. You don't need to say sorry. You have done nothing wrong dear, don't be afraid. I'm here with you. You don't need to cry or worry".

Coming out of the tangle of the tape, Casey hugged Clark and calmed him down.

“I’ll go and call David back mom. There’s no need to call anyone now. He must be out waiting for me”.

“Listen Clark, let him be there, it’s fine. There’s no worrying about it. Let me handle this now. Let us get out. I need to show you something”

“What’s that mom?”

“You will find out soon, dear”.

CHAPTER SIX

THE CONFRONTATION

“Take this lantern and come with me”

“Where are we going mom? Are we going to look for David?”

Casey didn’t answered Clark’s question and opened the door to go out. Clark followed him. A minute later they were in the fields and Clark now knew where they were heading. A bit of hesitation going in that direction was clearly on his face. An unclear fear, with a mix of hesitation makes the situation more tense to move forward for anyone, let alone a small kid.

“Why are we going to the barn mom? Is David there inside?”

Though Clark was asking for the clarity, he was himself not clear whether why fear has suddenly surrounded him going to the barn. A few days back, he was curious to know what was inside there, even when his mother told him not to go there, and now he was struggling to take steps, like something has happened to his legs, when his mother was taking him there. It was unclear whether it was a fear of seeing something unusual, like his mom being trapped there and the one with whom he is going there turns out to be someone who wants to take her place, as he was still in two minds to a certain extent, OR his mother making him stay there locked as a punishment for what he has done to her.

"Come with me" Casey unlocked the door of the barn. Though it was still day outside but it was dark there inside. The floor of the barn was covered, almost stuffed with hay. Casey lit the lamp and the barn was filled with the light of it. Almost at the center of it, an attic was built with a small kind of hut, probably for the kids.

Clark seeing the barn, memories of the past flashed through his mind. Playing in the fields with David, in the attic inside the toy house while Casey and Roger were busy in their work in the barn, all seemed to be the things of just yesterday. But suddenly, the fear came back on his face.

"Come on dear, climb up. Don't worry I'm here with you" Casey assured her.

Slowly and steadily Clark climbed the ladder up the attic. It was some 20-25 feet high above the ground. On it there was a toy house, which was built for Clark and David when they were kids. Color books, crayons, comic books, toys were there kept at one side of the attic. They were for them when they were kids.

"Clark, I want to tell you something. You need to hear it patiently and understand. And remember, you have done nothing wrong.

David is no more with us now. He is dead, he died long ago when you were small. You both were playing here and suddenly while playing you....it was just an accident dear, it wasn't your fault at all".

"No you are lying, he is here hiding somewhere, we should go and find him". Clark dismissing what Casey was telling him.

"Listen dear, you need to understand this. Its time that you should see the truth, I know it is hard for you but this is the truth. Your dad and I, decided to take you away from here, so that the bad memories don't haunt you. We both decided to part our ways, so that what happened, doesn't affects you and your future. But now I think, its time that I should tell you all this. You need to let go him of your memories. He does not belong to be here. Clark, dear....you have to..."

"No, you're lying, its not true, you're lying, just go away...leave me alone"

A sudden push from Clark to Casey in a fit of anger, not believing to what she just said. She came crashing down the attic, head first on the floor. It was an instant death. Clark still not able to believe the words of Casey, was shocked to what just happened. The hay lying all over the barn caught fire with the fire from the lantern which broke when Casey came crashing. All this, made Clark come to his senses. He quickly came down from the attic for his mother.

"Mom. Get up. Its fire here all around. We need to get out of here. Mom, get up."

It was of no use now. Clark with fear and a heavy heart, sobbing, came out of the barn and started running away from it. He ran as fast as he could, if his life was at risk, running away from the fire or from the reality he just faced, only he could tell. Exhausted and feeling hard to catch his breath, he stopped after running a good distance away from there.

He was crying, he was all alone, no one to console him, no one to tell him that it will be alright. He closed his eyes. The sun was shining brightly, it was still afternoon.

"Clark, dear..."

The sound was very much familiar to Clark. He opened his eyes. Casey was standing in front of him. David was also beside Casey.

"Mom...." He could say nothing else.

"You have done nothing wrong my child, don't worry, I have always there for you" and she raised her hands towards him.

Just like an innocent child who knows nothing about the world, Clark happily holds her hands, follows her with David beside him, knowing that nothing will ever happen to him until his mom is with him. The fire was still alit inside the barn but the heat of the sun looked far more brighter and the three shadows could be seen going far from it, fading every moment.

There was a complete silence in the room. All glued to the story and the characters which was broken by the words of professor

"So, that's it. Here is the end of the story"

"Professor, can I ask you one thing?"

"Yes. Go ahead"

"If David was dead. Why did Clark behaved as if he can see him and what made him behave like that with his mother?"

"Clark was suffering from what we call in medical terms 'Bereavement hallucination'. David was his only and first friend he encountered in his life, with whom he shared everything. It happens that if someone close to you passes away, who was very dear to you, you still happen to see them and even talk to them, while in actual they are not there. Clark was too small to understand all this, which is why his parents thought to move him from where it all happened and avoided any medication for such.

Now as far as his behavior is concerned, when you have twins, being a parent you equally share your love on the kids but one or the other always thinks that he is getting less attention from them. In this case it was David who used to think it that way while he was alive. So whenever, Clark thought that he was talking to David, his brain was actually responding as to how David might be thinking the things his way. This led to Clark think in the negative way towards his mother Casey. You might call this type of functioning of the brain, a miracle, but it happens in many ways and sometimes work wonders."

"Professor, is this just a story or is there any truth in it?"

"Well, it depends on you. If you believe in it, then it is a reality otherwise it is a story for you".

Ywg.official

Young Writers Group (YWG.OFFICIAL) is an organisation which is working to help writers in showcasing their work in front of vast number of readers . We offers a budget friendly packages to our writers. We are working as a writer's helping society. You can have a talk with us regarding publishing your book on our instagram :@YWG.OFFICIAL
Or you can drop your mail on ywg.co.in@gmail.com
Else you can also contact us on following numbers
Akash: 7404390981
Aashika: 9634644516

9 798888 696576

Printed by Libri Plureos GmbH in Hamburg, Germany